Why Can't Meatballs Sleep?

Titus O'Neil

BookLeaf Publishing

India | USA | UK

Why Can't Meatballs Sleep? © 2023 Titus O'Neil

All rights reserved.

No part of this publication may be reproduced, stored in a retrieval system, or transmitted, in any form or by any means, electronic, mechanical, photocopying, recording, or otherwise, without the prior written permission of the presenters.

Titus O'Neil asserts the moral right to be identified as the author of this work.

Presentation by *BookLeaf Publishing*

Web: www.bookleafpub.com

E-mail: info@bookleafpub.com

ISBN: 9789357696067

First edition 2023

For the extra sauce left in the pan overnight

Involuntary Insomniac

Budding youth
Full of eagerness and curiosity
I don't know when it happened
But I was really young
When I needed to stay awake
To flip to side B of the tape

Three dreams
Each night plaguing and haunting
Perhaps they played a part
Causing my evasive slumber
Or merely recurring nightmares
Following my dreams for years

Be better
Attacking me from every angle
This senseless notion that I
Was to be above the others
As if the guilt of simply having thought
Wasn't enough to keep my rest caught

Boot camp
And all after basic training
Waiting for him to go to war
Crying alone in top bunk darkness

That was the first time I felt
Sure I could never sleep that well

Years alone
Not too many but enough
The solitude didn't seem like much
But imagination was my closest friend
Perhaps it was just that my life was boring
But I begged for sleep always imploring

First love
Or my idea of it
She staved off the feelings
For a time but only moments
Not too long before the cause became
Just another way to say her name

Second love
Or maybe the real first
I learned that spending the night
Next to another was enough
Forcing me to sleep for her sake
Maybe I'll learn that it's a mistake

Car crash
Stranded in bed for weeks
I sleep with drugs in my veins
Or since there's nothing else to do
But later the regrets that creep

Can ensure that I will never sleep

Third love
Probably the only real one
It lasted too long and I suppose
That should have been my first warning
Sleeping that much after all this time
Should have shouted that nothing was fine

Lifetimes pass
Restful nights become too elusive
It's at this point that I begin to understand
This plague is my own doing my own desire
Slumber is something for proper people
Not for regrets that seem unspeakable

Everything's fine
I have nothing to complain
But every little problem can set off
This conviction of my self-punishment
Everything I feel just festers deep
I don't think that I want to sleep

I stay awake. Thinking…

I can't get out of Pennsylvania

There is a dragon stagnantly lying
        under Pennsylvania
It snores flames instead of flying
        in the mines of Centralia
Thick fog of morning, the smoke it exhales
        that settles in the valleys
The rolling hills are its flaking scales
        molting into earthy alleys
Shores along Lake Erie
        mark the wings where they fringe
While the state university
        sits where those same wings hinge
Buildings of Philadelphia, tower
        as the spines along its neck
Should it wake, it will devour
        until there is nothing left
Pittsburgh steel, each in number
        are its plated tail in order
Stretching its claws in its slumber
        caused the ragged Jersey border
Earth of the state will heave
        each time a breath is drawn
The steamy air beneath
        scorches every manicured lawn

This legend stirs every now and then
            but it cannot escape its home
In the next millennia, it will try again
            until it is finally free to roam

Little Meatball Lies

Mr. Meatball says to his son
Sit still or the sauce will miss you
But Little Meatball can't stay still
There's too much to be done

He rolls around
His father scolds
No one wants you
If you don't do what you're told

Little Meatball wants to be great
And as big as his old man
He discovers the trick to flight
And soars off the ceramic plate

At first he eats the roof
Wood beams insulation and shingles
But he just can't seem to stop
The taste of the household mingles

Barely filling for such a Meatball
He reaches the clouds and dines
The snowflakes are better
But wetter and not enough at all

Crashing through the atmosphere
Little Meatball ascends into space
What morsels can he consume here
As he wipes ozone off his face

He bumps an asteroid by happenstance
Little Meatball eats it away
Chewing a meteor to get meatier
This is finally his great chance

But he made one mistake
With all his crazy snacking
He didn't get too far away and
Gravity pulls him back in

The reentry causes his new form to melt
He becomes Little Meatball again
As he lands back on the plate
Dissatisfied with this hand he was dealt

He tells his father exactly what happened
Weaving the tale to its end
But Mr. Meatball shakes it all off
And scolds him once again

You're dry as a bone for one simple fact
You can't sit still for a moment
And now here you are as you were
So dry that you're barely intact

Flamingo

I guess I'll face toward you tonight.
I don't really know if I did last night.
I don't remember if I wake up anymore,
But I used to with you.
I would always remember how I fell asleep,
And how I woke up with you beside me.
Strangely, my arm never fell asleep as much.
I never seemed to have trouble
Falling asleep with you.
It must be because you were exhausting.
But it's hard to sleep now.

The good news is, I've replaced you.
Someone gave me this stuffed toy,
And it pushes on my back at night
The way that maybe you did.
It feels right for it to be there,
But I suppose it's only a substitution.
How long until I replace that.
Maybe I'll just get a dog.

Sleepless Seas

Waves lapping, ceaseless
Surging thoughts keep me awake
Oceans never sleep

Ripple
Ripple
Roaring waves
Crash upon the craggy rock
Surf across the sand
Running endlessly
In each direction
Further than can be seen
Toss a stone into a lake
Its ripples reach the shore
The moon is just a giant stone
Causing giant ripples forevermore

What do they matter
Thoughts running like an ocean
I can barely swim

Ghyse: A Sea Shanty

To depths unknown and back again
Stay true to crew, he'll be your friend
But if you cross him, it's your end
They call him Captain Ghyse

He seeks out all the world's thrills
His crew will do whatever he wills
He takes no prisoners, only kills
That fearsome, Captain Ghyse

Forget yourself before his power
His foes can only grovel and cower
He'll come for you at any hour
That terror, Captain Ghyse

The lord of death allowed him live
To take whatever he can give
But still the booty we can div-
-ide from generous Ghyse

He sends the souls to keep his own
His name throughout the world is known
His conquering power is always shown
The mighty Captain Ghyse

The ghost that floats all o'er the seas
He'll drop you down onto your knees
And even if you beg him please...
You're killed by ruthless Ghyse

Perhaps someday he'll rot away
But his terror will always stay
I'm sure he'll come back anyway
That legend, old Captain Ghyse

Little Meatball Tries

Little Meatball loves so big
Bigger than any meatball
He could ever be
But then he can't love wide

Little Meatball loves so wide
Wider than any plate
He could ever live on
But then he can't love big

Little Meatball focuses on others
Every meatball, noodle, and tomato
That live on his plate with him
But then he can't focus on himself

Little Meatball focuses on himself
Each part that he finds wrong
He tries to let himself be happy
But then he can't focus on others

Little Meatball is selfless
To the point where it's a fault
Little Meatball is selfish
To the point where it's a fault

Little Meatball is confused
Everyone seems conflicted about him
But not as much as Little Meatball
He's never felt a different way

My Heart as a Soda Can

Fizz and crackle
The sound of so many things
A rattle of rain
Unsoggy cereal
A fitful fire
Carbonation in a can
Snow snuggling in with its kin
Can a heart fizz and crackle?
I'd like to believe it can

My heart will fizz and crackle
Hearing the mention of your name
But to speak with you is something new
More like an explosion in my vein
Than some little noise in my brain

O'Neil

The ninth in line
Heir to nothing
Save the heartache and
Guilts you all left our mother

Nothing expected yet
All hopes are pinned
Perhaps of my own imagination
Perhaps of your regrets

Protected and protector
The weakest yet strong
A confidant to each
Though the last thing I want

My memory mostly fabricated
Twisted like a TV script
Barely any my own since
I was never born yet

You say I was spoiled
But I say it differently
When I reached the age to
See what you truly were

Still our unspoken love
It tangles both ways
The bindings of our blood
Devoting us to each other

Before

Remember when the birds sang and it sounded right
The singing that sank into your consciousness
As you felt invigorated and more in tune with yourself
Those first few times in the woods
Before those sounds became the droning and
The noise that looped long after you fall asleep

When the wind rustled leaves crunched together at the gentlest touch and
It didn't mean pumpkin spice and flannels
When the snowfall in the light of the streetlamp beyond
The dark veil of the six o'clock phone call
Made you so awake that you couldn't get your boots and gloves on fast enough
When the snooze button was only made for buses

A rainy day used to only mean rubber boots and a jacket instead of
An umbrella opening depression above your head

 Full of hair that you just can't seem to style
quite right
 When a hot summer day simply meant standing
in front of a fan for a moment
 Saying the silliest thought in your wandering
mind into
 The blades as they spun the words around
before throwing them back at you

 Those days filled with life
 The bird song was your breath
 The crickets' chirp your heartbeat
 The fireflies were your pulse
 And you ran through the cornfield
 Faster than the nerves in your brain

Danse of the Skeletal Skyscraper

You can make it reach if you only try hard
enough
Try harder than the bones you piece together
The moss-covered
The broken and fractured
The yellowed and bowed
The disformed and dirtied
The bones that you found
Some with bits of flesh
Some with teeth marks in them
The bones you dug up
That you pulled out of the weeds
That you pulled out of others
Connect them
Touch the joints together
Make the fractured bits line up with their best
match
Burrow out the marrow to squish the glues in
the hollows
But the glue is not needed
The bones want to be together

The natural twists and knobs
Helix and gnarl in a way that tells you its own
shape
The sizes may differ as the creatures they come
from
But that's what makes the structure unique
Cross brace and bracket
Anchor and fasten
These bones have a way to go
The moon is not so far
But that will only serve to stabilize it
Piece by piece
Link and splice
Rung by rung like a ladder
You craft and assemble
Like some macabre macrame
What started as practical has become an art
The splintered bits lace out
With lesser bones adding adornment
Fish bones
Bird bones
Lizards and snakes
Phalanges and Metatarsals
Jutting out like the moorings of a web
The discolored and blemished
Seem to twinkle in the moonlight
As its silvered shadows shapeshift with the
clouds

The ghouls begin to stir
Taking notice of your monumental feature
They mindlessly circle like a vomitous huddle
Unable to think they begin to gnaw
Some on the grass
Some on the trees and vines
Others on their fellow fiends
But some mash their remnants of teeth
Into the bones
But you pay them no mind
The moon is getting so close you can see its
pores
The gumming of ghouls continues
And they begin to push the base about
Causing the structure to sway
Like a dance of the bewitching bones
The tallest trees stretch their branches
They wrap their timber tendrils around the
bones
Shoring them up as you continue to construct
The ghosts emerge in intrigue of the skyscraper
Some possess the ghouls to stop their gnashing
But the bones still bounce
Dancing in the whispers of the wind

Scaling the skeleton frame
You can only just touch the moon
So many bones to get this far
So many more needed to go beyond
Touching back down to the earth
You look back at the moon
And the field of stars where it nestles
As you lay the next few pieces
Bolstering into the moon
You step out onto its craters
You gaze again at the heavens
The closest you have ever been
Reaching out your hand
Stars contort and twist in a maniacal manner
Until they have all joined together to form
A skull to match the bones you've built
The heavens are starving
All you have are bones
A meal that satisfies no one
They begin to inhale
Stripping away your skin
You unravel away like a bandage
Raw and barren as only muscle and tendons
The stars continue to breathe your flesh away
Strings and ribbons of your being sail
Into the black ocean speckled with lights
This small morsel of human
Leaves them only wanting more

The ladder of bone continues to dance
The silent song now nearly screaming
You reach down and grasp
In your new skeleton form
Your face a reflection of the ravenous
constellation above
Begin hoisting as hard as you can
Bone by bone by bone
You raise your skyscraper heavenward
Replanting it on the lunar surface
Climbing once again
You scale and scour
No longer knowing what lies ahead
Reaching the top of this construct
You feel no closer than you were before
Raise your bony hand
Grasp and clutch at the starry skull no closer
The white of your bones
Begins to powder and flow into that blackness
Dusting the endlessness with more lights
Made from you
Your skeleton skyscraper sways beneath you
Though there is no more breeze
You cannot reach the stars
They may not even be real
The skull constellation releases itself
Back to the dot dappled eternity
As your full form evaporates
You steal a glance at your creation

The bones you pieced together
Meet the same fate as you
The bones want to be together
The heavens are starving
And they eat you whole

Little Meatball Cries

Little meatball is leaking tears
Or perhaps it's just excess grease
He doesn't know why he feels sad
But this dripping fluid is a release

Don't be sad Little Meatball
Mr. Meatball tries to console
But what good are these words
For a heart so heavy and full

It doesn't last all that long
After he reaches his greasy limit
Time is all that can make him better
Little Meatball just needs a minute

Porcelain Onions

Smash.
The pieces shatter
Scatter
Clattering along the sidewalk.
Some dust floats from pieces that stay
While others skitter to the grass away.

A strange onion one out of maybe a dozen
Gifted to you by the one who made you smash
them
He took something from you one out of maybe
nine
But each of those nine is a ninth of your life

Shout.
Your voice raises
Rages
Grating as your lungs breathe in the dust.
The pain in your voice can't compare
To the pain that festers as your despair.

I can't cry the way you do
But I want to
I share the hurt you have in your heart

But I don't share the blame you place on
yourself
I'm numb and I need to hide within myself
You feel it all and need to let it out

Crash.
The second goes
Explodes
Throwing its shards about.
A simple ornament to sit in your garden
The sound of its shattering is your angry jargon.

Each sliver a piece of your crumbling heart
Resting where only the worms will find them
In the end you bury them deeper
No one will speak of this again

Rage.
Our hearts knobbing
Throbbing
Fogging up our vision.
We were robbed of someone without a choice
He told us himself with his cracking voice.

It's your fault you think
as you smash the next on the stones
It's your fault you think
of the manipulator that left us stranded alone
It's your fault you think…

that the onion will take your blame

I see the dust but only for a moment
I see your rage in the same way
The love so deep that it could drive you to this
Clouded over by the rasp of your screams

Scream.
One of many a profanity
Insanity
Christianity avoids the F one.
The clatter of porcelain finally diminished
As the absence of whole bulbs reveals you are
finished.

I want to speak
To say I love you
I'm not sure which one I mean
So I watch as you simply walk
Back into the house where he won't be

Goblin Love

They ran along the shoreline
As lovers are meant to do
Hand in hand
Gliding over the sand
While they called each other mine.

Their eyes bulging as they gaze
Into the eyes of the one they love
To feel this way must be forbidden.
Jagged teeth gnarl out of their lips
Revealed by their crooked smiles
The lapping waves sing sweetly
Caught by the lovers' ears
Which twist and curl
In such peculiar ways
That they could be mistaken
For some special pastry
But neither mind
This is all they want.
They finally stopped
They could no longer help it
The feeling was too great
A kiss exchanged
As their knobbed noses
Hooked to form a new shape

To feel this way must be forbidden.
This is all they want.

The man came down the shoreline
As a hunter stalking prey
The arrows nocked
His sights now locked
And he ended their love's time.

Packing means I will never unpack

It's numbing to think
That all our lives
Can fit into garbage bags
Or bins and boxes alike
We compact and compartment
Each of our beings
Into little containers for storage
And ship them wherever we decide
Just load up the truck
Shut the door like the lids
Close the house door
And hand the keys over
As you take your identity somewhere else
What a grand adventure it could be
So why does it hurt so much

I stop myself from leaving Pennsylvania

Sling myself up over the wall
It doesn't matter how hard I fall
I'll land so soft
Like clouds aloft
I'm ready to battle on

Surrounding me, the flames of myth
I hasten on through them forthwith
Slay the beast
Or wound at least
As he tries to travel on

My comrades, wounded, struggle to rise
As the fearsome foe rages and cries
Its roar is deafening
Morale is lessening
In fear, they prattle on

Raise my blade, heroically shout
Self-declare my warrior clout
Prepare to strike
Brandish my knife
Its splendor rivaling Babylon

To beat a legend, I fight with a fable
The only sword that can be capable
To finish this wyrm
My grip is firm
Time for doubt is now forgone

I march toward this creature of rage
I must return it to its earthen cage
It grits its teeth
And drops beneath
The land quakes and rattles on

The fight begins, clawing and flames spitting
I slash its solid hide and keep on hitting
The battle is fierce
I can barely pierce
This exchange goes on to dawn

Exhausted, I struggle to strike anymore
But I cannot lose like I did before
The fiend is weakened
My conviction, deepened
No matter what, I must carry on

One final attack as the monster lurches
I leap and land, as my blade finds purchase
Bury the sword
Striking earthward
Ending this violent marathon

The dragon finally having felt defeat
Begins its disgraceful, wounded retreat
Back to its lair for a long recovery
Someday to be a new discovery
Under Pennsylvania
Another millennia
For the imprisoned to live on

Only Child Orphan

They sleep beneath
A nice reprieve
I walk above
Just showing off
All they can do is rest
I can only nap at best
They didn't ask for lack of life
I didn't ask for sleepless strife
All of them, gone already
Making my burden heavy
Ten interred under one family name
How haunting that I must share the same
I've always assumed I'd watch you pass
Even so, this pain will last
I can't describe how much I hurt
While you lay surrounded by dirt
Eternally embraced by the earth
The first to hold me after birth
I don't stand a chance in this life alone
But you all left and stole my home
Now I wish for only one thing
To cease to count among the living

Little Meatball Dies

Little Meatball is restless.
When will he be devoured?
As the noodles pass,
He is saved for last.
He hopes his flavor has soured.

Little Meatball is stabbed.
His entire body run through.
A toothpick raises him.
A wet tongue cradles him.
His end is coming true.

Little Meatball is ravaged.
Molars mash his body apart.
As each bit is swallowed,
The mouth is hollowed.
He's gone without a remark.

Obligatory poem about someone generically specific or specifically generic: Yes, it's about you.

Dark pools of honey
Swirling like a solar system
They take on the guise
Of resplendent eyes
I can't comprehend how
So many have missed them

They draw me in
As a comet in your gravitation
I would be remiss
To get lost in your irises
When all your features
Are deserving of such adoration

Whether wanted or not
Your presence is a constant
My version of you in my conscience
Could be nothing more than nonsense
I cannot push it away
Without feeling hollow and despondent

I won't say I love you
But I know that is my goal
To love someone without any condition
Is to forget yourself without permission
I'll forget myself everyday
And worship you as an idol
:)

Please.

just let me go
          even though you aren't holding on
                    no matter what i do
                              i'm always completely
                    wrong

you're in my head
          even though i don't know you
                    when all i wanted
                              was a chance to get
                              close to you

Little Meatball Rise

Smashed apart
Like a broken heart
He clings alive
Refusing to drift away
He'll clamor
Gooping himself back together

He's formless
Like a god and no less
He shapes himself
In whatever image he chooses
He'll morph
Nothing can hold him back

Forced fight
Like a plant for light
He brawls about
Battling his way out
He'll eject
Rocketing himself back to the world

He's unfettered
Like an envelope unlettered
He crashes down
Into the world that destroyed him

He'll unleash
Leaving all he knew in ruin

Unstoppable force
Like the ocean's course
He wanders away
Leaving nothing in his wake
He'll forget
Everything that used to contain him

The table
The plate
The pasta
The sauce
Even Mr. Meatball

Voluntary Insomniac

Most days
I feel lost and crazy
It may be my own doing
Or some chemical imbalance
But this sinking in my chest
Is more than simple restlessness

Worry always
Thinking for You and me
I take responsibility for both
Your thoughts and actions and mine
But the responsibility should be Yours
As my mind wanders cobwebbed corridors

Recall regret
Never let it go away
Each regret juts and pierces
I've crafted a cage of thorns
Nestling its briars into my brain
Recall them again without restrain

Plan ahead
I play out every possibility
Demanding myself do it over
If the outcome is wrong

I attempt to stitch my dreams together
But no dreams without sleep remember

One person
Shouldn't have so much power
You may change but this remains
I hate the way You make me feel
I bet I don't even cross Your mind
When You are the only thing on mine

Mirrors around
Are You next to me
I don't know who I'm talking to
And I don't know who to blame
My mind is split in fragmentation
Down the twisting halls of imagination

Haunt me
Each You that ever existed
I deserve to be crushed
By guilt and depression
I hope You all kept the piece of heart
That I foolishly gave You from the start

Destroy me
Burn my heart to ash
I forced it on You without permission
Some of You not even knowing you have it
I can only hope at this point I'm hollow

So there won't be another You to follow

Love me
Either You or someone new
I have proven I can't be the one
To keep myself happy and asleep
Someone gather my heart back in my chest
Hold me so tight that I finally rest

Let me stop thinking…

www.ingramcontent.com/pod-product-compliance
Lightning Source LLC
LaVergne TN
LVHW021314200726
843509LV00012B/1909